Mama, Will God Still Love Me?

Written By: Cindy Schneiderman

Illustrated By: Tarah Wise

Published by
Hasmark Publishing, judy@hasmarkservices.com

Disclaimer

This book is designed to provide information and motivation to our readers. It is sold with the understanding that the publisher is not engaged to render any type of psychological, legal, or any other kind of professional advice. The content of each article is the sole expression and opinion of its author, and not necessarily that of the publisher. No warranties or guarantees are expressed or implied by the publisher's choice to include any of the content in this volume. Neither the publisher nor the individual author(s) shall be liable for any physical, psychological, emotional, financial, or commercial damages, including, but not limited to, special, incidental, consequential or other damages. Our views and rights are the same: You are responsible for your own choices, actions, and results.

Permission should be addressed in writing to Cindy Schneiderman at gmagrace4@gmail.com

Editor: Becky Crane
rcranefl@yahoo.com

Illustrator: Tarah Wise
gmagrace4@gmail.com

Book Layout: Anne Karklins
annekarklins@gmail.com

ISBN-13: 978-1-988071-95-4
ISBN-10: 198807195X

Hasmark
PUBLISHING

To my Grandchildren,

May you always feel God's unfailing love.
May you know that he is guiding you throughout your life.
His love endures forever!

I LOVE YOU!!!

Grandma

"Mama, will
God still love me if
I break all my crayons?"

"Yes, Little Bear,
God will still love you
if you break
all your Crayons."

"Mama, will
God still love me if
I fight with
my sister?"

"Yes, Little Bear,
God will still love you
if you fight
with your sister."

"Mama, will
God still love me if
I stomp my feet
and cry?"

"Yes, Little Bear,
God will still love you
if you stomp your feet
and cry."

"Mama, will
God still love me if
I don't listen
to you and Papa?"

"Yes, Little Bear,
God will still love you
if you don't listen to
me and Papa."

"Little Bear,
God will still love you
no matter what you do,
because, my son,
God created you!"

Psalm 52:8b

"I trust in God's
unfailing love forever."

About the Author

Cindy is a mother of five and a grandmother of five. She and her husband Bob enjoy spending time with all of their children and grandchildren. When they get together it is always a fun-filled day!

Cindy grew up in a small town of 600 people in Illinois. She enjoys sharing God's love with everyone. Cindy decided to write, *Mama, Will God Still Love Me* when she watched her children's and grand-children's love for God grow, along with their questions. She wanted them to know that God is always listening and loves them unconditionally. She knew that many people would benefit knowing God's love, so she decided to share this story with others.

Cindy enjoys inspiring and helping others to know they can do and be whatever they want in life. In fact, when the Grandchildren share their goals with her, she joyously says, "You can do it!"

Matthew 19:26
"With God all things are possible."

About the Illustrator

Tarah is 12 years old and the granddaughter of the author. She is also the middle of three children. Tarah loves to draw! When her grandmother asked her to draw the pages for this book she immediately jumped into action, sending back sketches for her grandmother to add to the book.

She won the yearbook cover at her school out of many children, and can often be found drawing many different cartoon characters. This is the first book Tarah has "officially" illustrated, however, we expect many more in her future. When Tarah isn't drawing she is very active in gymnastics and track. She also loves all animals, spending many hours chasing them around her grandparents farm.